HarperCollins*Publishers*
1 London Bridge Street
London SE1 9GF

www.harpercollins.co.uk

First published by HarperCollins*Publishers* 2020

10 9 8 7 6 5 4 3 2 1

A catalogue record of this book is available from the British Library

ISBN 978-0-00-840908-1

Printed and bound by PNB Latvia

OK
BOOMER

'What time is that on Netflix?'

AND OTHER DAILY STRUGGLES

 HarperCollins*Publishers*

CONTENTS

DISCLAIMER: NOT ALL BABY BOOMERS ARE BOOMERS. BOOMER IS A STATE OF MIND.

Everywhere you go, there are Boomers. School, college, uni, work, home – they've got all bases covered.

Some are *actual* baby boomers who spend their days driving SUVs, buying up property, printing out their emails, denying climate change, supporting gender stereotypes and loudly denouncing everybody who disagrees with them.

Some don't even look old enough to *be* baby boomers – that's because they're not, but if they adhere to any of the above behaviours, we give you permission to call them out on it. All. Day. Long. (Those guys are the worst.)

For YEARS we searched high and low for a suitably pithy put-down to end all unnecessary arguments – to stun, surprise and slay. To assert our authority and succinctly suggest that maybe, just maybe, the older generations don't have all the answers.

And *finally*, Mother Internet provided.

This collection is a snapshot of the very best uses of 'OK Boomer' on the Internet … which we've printed … for ease … and for fun … Perhaps there's a bit of Boomer in all of us. We hope you find solace in these pages.*

*If you're a Boomer reading this, the first step to recovery is recognition. There's still time to change. We hope this helps.

Every time an angry baby boomer misspells millennial, an angel gets its student loans forgiven.

@jaboukie 13 May

1

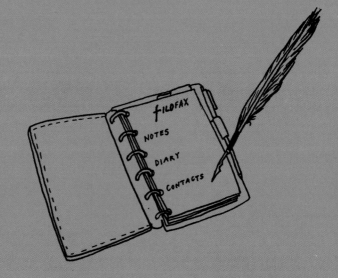

WHO ARE YOU CALLING A BOOMER?

Boomer mentality is being dismissive of anybody who disagrees with you, without properly checking the facts. It's voicing outdated opinions or inaccurate information such as:

'YOU, SON, SHOULD NOT BE WEARING PINK'

or
'KIDS TODAY ARE TOO SENSITIVE'

or
'YOU WON'T GET A JOB WITH THAT TATTOO'

or
'GENERATION Z HAS IT SO EASY'

If you have said any of the above statements or similar, you are a Boomer. Dig out that Filofax and start taking notes!

The peasants hath become accustomed to speaking a most detestable phrase: 'AS YOU SAY, ELDER.' They utter it with a most indecent tone, implying disbelief and rebellious sentiments. This phrase might rightly be compared to the gravest insult of our age, which I dare not write.

@historybro 14 Nov

If you can't deal with the postmodern madness of 'Boomer is a mentality, not an age' then you may, in fact, be a Boomer.

@esj312 30 Jan

Avocado tastes better mixed with baby boomer tears, pass it on.

@alice 9 Jun

Baby boomer voice 'Kids today are too soft. In MY day we were emotionally abused by our parents and we repressed our trauma so deeply we incorporated that abuse into a toxic system of values that prize a mythological "toughness" at the expense of actually dealing with our pain.'

@elle_em 24 Jun

When you say 'OK Boomer' to a Boomer, make sure you speak loudly and clearly.

@CanyonDentalCen 28 Jan

Anyone that still replies to emails and keeps the 'sent from my iPhone' tag is clearly a Boomer.

@luftherz 4 Feb

Just had a Boomer lady at the vet's office come up to me and say, 'I like your ink! I got a few myself' and I shit you not she showed me a minion tattoo on her arm.

@SloughWitch 14 Nov

Broke:

Saying OK BOOMER to actual Boomers

Woke:

Saying OK BOOMER to anyone who disagrees with you, regardless of age

@mkvdub95 11 Feb

Argument with:

Person older than you:
OK Boomer

Dog beautician:
OK Groomer

Piano technician:
OK Tuner

Frank Sinatra:
OK Crooner

Buzz Aldrin:
OK Mooner

Weaver:
OK Loomer

Fish:
OK Tuna

Boat:
OK Schooner

Robotic vacuum:
OK Roomba

@Swan_Corleone2 21 Jan

2

THE NATURAL WORLD

Don't get us wrong, we *love* the feeling of new clothes, the cosiness of log fires, the sense of adventure that comes with long-haul flights, the surprise of fireworks, the comfort of big cars, the convenience of disposable cups, the effortlessness of online deliveries and the pop-pop-popping of bubble wrap ... But do you know what we'd prefer?

A functioning planet.

**Millennial:
I wanna die
Boomer:
Here's climate change
Millennial:
Not like that**

@robots_feel 3 Feb

**Me: If we don't
immediately halt the
use of fossil fuels,
I won't live to be 40
Baby Boomer:
OK, but that could really
hurt my career**

@SydneyAzari 16 Nov

22

Boomer:
Climate change doesn't exist

Me:
Nice nursing homes don't exist 😜

@KieranMSimpson 15 Jan

Boomer is no longer an age.
It is a state of mind. If a 26yo
tells you Greta Thunberg seems
like an idiot, you're legally
obligated to say 'OK Boomer'
And put them in a home 😂😂😂

@Skoog 8 Oct

Overheard in the library:
Student One: *Marches over to
the non-fiction section, returns
bearing Greta's book*
Student Two, in response:
I refuse to let anyone tell me
what I should and shouldn't do
Student One: OK Boomer

@mischelej 30 Jan

SO I ALWAYS GREW
UP WITH OLDER
GENERATIONS TELLING
ME HOW EPIC THEIR
WINTERS WERE WHEN
THEY WERE YOUNGER.
NOW THEY TELL ME
GLOBAL WARMING IS
FAKE. YET WHERE IS ALL
THE SNOW OF YOUR
YOUTH, KAREN?!??!?

#GlobalWarming
#OKBoomer
#itsrealdammit

@threewhiskeysd1 30 Jan

Geez I hate these greenies!! All they want to do is save the planet so my children and grandchildren have clean air and water and a habitable home. Why do they like everyone so much? It's like everyone is equal or something??? #OKBoomer ✊🏻✊🏼✊🏽

@reneelsamson 4 Feb

Boomer:
I'll be dead before climate change is an issue

Me:
You'll be dead before I regret my tattoo but you won't stfu about that

@robots_feel 14 Jan

Baby boomers are always like 'Did you put those holes in your jeans yourself?'
I DON'T KNOW, SUSAN, DID YOU PUT THE HOLE IN THE OZONE THERE YOURSELF?

@rnariegallagher 24 Mar

Boomers on a 65-degree day in January:

'How strange! Let's go out and enjoy it!'

Millennials on a 65-degree day in January:

'Oh god, oh god, oh god, oh god, oh god …'

@rhinosoros 12 Jan

3

LOVE

It seems romance has changed since baby boomer times. From the way they talk about their spouses, anyone would think they'd spent their whole lives bottling up their feelings, avoiding therapy and masking all emotional pain with their disposable income.

It *sounds* like some bought big houses and cars, fancy jewellery and holidays. And now they sit bejewelled in their mansions, with Range Rovers on the driveways, surrounded by glossy holiday photographs, quietly contemplating what they ever saw in their partners and how they ended up here …

And they *really* want you to do the same.

#HappyEverAfter

Boomer:
Lmao why aren't these millennials getting married? I married my sweetheart as soon as we left high school!

Also Boomer:
I hate my wife

@human-dlc 3 Oct

My dad just told me to smile to get men to like me … #OKBoomer

@linkiverdi 5 Feb

My dad just asked 'Why are you on your phone?' I snapped back 'I'm WORKING' because that's quicker than explaining I have to keep rewatching this video of my ex kissing some girl I found on a stranger's insta until I stop feeling anything at all lol wow Boomers just don't get it

@HarperRoseD 16 Jan

When the Boomer love song playing is REALLY putting emphasis on 'little girl'

@PatsSheep 15 Jan

Boomers like 'while you sit there reading a book on your phone for this entire train ride I, an intellectual, stare into the middle distance and have one long 45-minute think about how I hate my wife and kids.'

@brushykb 24 Jan

Boomers get so worked up over Facebook selling their information as if Russia is gonna be able to do anything sinister with the knowledge of their failing marriage and coffee memes.

@RealYungCripp 25 Jan

FIRST I DRINK THE COFFEE, THEN I DO THE STUFF.

I just OK Boomer'd my boyfriend (he's 4 years older than me) and I shit you not he looked at me like

@tenzohoe 13 Feb

Pretty sure my dad asks me when Valentine's Day is every year …? #OKBoomer

@AylaMusic 5 Feb

Dating guys who don't use social media is so peaceful. They don't care about 'bomboclat' or 'OK Boomer' or 'our impending war with Iran' they just wanna talk about their new instant pot and how fast it cooks rice.

@sumbdkut 18 Jan

There should be a new dating app like 'OK Cupid' but for old people called 'OK Boomer' ...

@brainwxrms 14 Oct

OK I think I cracked the code
Boomers: I hate my wife
Gen X: My wife left me
Millennials: I love my wife

@TheSocietyDude 11 Feb

4

I can't work out where the cable goes for the wireless

I remember that it's Ctrl+C, but what comes next?

TECH-NOLOGY

It's funny how Boomers are always telling us how the world works, but they haven't yet figured out how Word works …

Growing up in a tech-savvy age has many advantages. The one disadvantage, however, is that you immediately adopt the role of 'Tech Genius' in your family and workplace the SECOND you reveal you know how to create a desktop shortcut.

Cue a lifetime of daily interruptions.

Don't worry, fellow Millennials, if a Baby Boomer is calling you 'too soft' or 'overly sensitive', just tell them you saw their identity for sale on the dark web.

@ellle_em 24 Apr

Baby Boomer: Just wait til you have to adapt to the real world, better start learnin' sweetie :)
Baby Boomer: *doesn't know how to copy/paste*

@rilbrego 24 Jan

'Smartphones are the root of evil'

OK Boomer, so go throw yours in the trash then.

@ns_zafri 31 Jan

HOW THE FUCK DID BOOMERS READ DINNER MENUS IN DIMLY LIT RESTAURANTS BEFORE FLASHLIGHT-EQUIPPED SMARTPHONES? #BOOMERFAIL

@BOOMERFAIL 16 SEP

WHEN ALL THE BOOMERS ARE DEAD DO Y'ALL WANNA CHANGE TO METRIC OR NAH?

@IMAGIMEEMEE 24 JAN

I keep waiting
for Alexa to
randomly retort
'OK Boomer'
after I ask it to
play a song or set
a cooking timer
or something

@lessin 20 Jan

Yesterday I walked past a 50+yr old woman describing to her friends her intricate Pokémon hatching schedule and planned pokestop route, all based around her walk to work. She's an OK Boomer.

@CateSpice 15 Jan

Only my second tweet ever.
Did I do it right?
#OKBoomer

@Go77Blue 5 Feb

Tonight I learned that Google
Home will respond to 'OK
Boomer' but then doesn't listen
to what you say.

@stchan11 24 Jan

Someone tell boomers in business to stop using 90s Microsoft Office smart objects. It's 2020, stop tiring my eyes.

@randomdirdy 5 Feb

Do you ever OK Boomer yourself? Just had an entire phone conversation that ended with me realizing I was asking questions to a voicemail and not, as I had assumed, an unresponsive man.

@Cuntillo 23 Jan

How telling is it that my grandmother genuinely believes that the storage on her phone directly impacts her battery life and signal … #Grandma #OKBoomer

@Hasepuckel 31 Jan

My co-worker told me about an older lady who asked desktop support if she could use #wd40 to lubricate her mouse! I almost died of laughter. This made my day. #TechSupport #OKBoomer #notajoke #IT #MondayVibes

@ChrisCalso 3 Feb

An 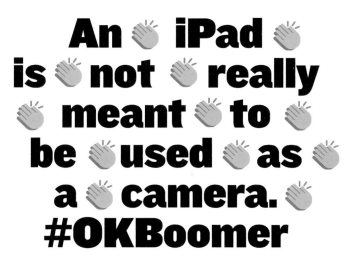 iPad is not really meant to be used as a camera. #OKBoomer

@khalilgarriott 30 Jan

5

WORKING LIFE

Getting one foot on the ladder and the other in the door can be a tricky balancing act that requires limitless patience.

Boomers – bless them – love to share their knowledge and experience of the world of work. Some of their advice can be useful, but most of it is hilariously confusing. The trick is to nod, smile, thank them and try to avoid laughing in their faces.

Boomer: 'Hand write and post a letter to the CEO – he will be so impressed by your rejection of modern technology.'

You: 'Really? It's a digital marketing role ... also FYI the CEO is a woman.'

TFW a co-worker brags about their extensive industry knowledge & treats you like their secretary while not knowing how to use the main software that's required of their job #OKBoomer

@ramanradhika01 4 Feb

Boomer boss:
We think of our business as like a family.

Millennial boss:
We think of our business as like a giant polycule.

Zoomer boss:
We think of our business as like an anime death cult.

@tgracchus1848 10 Jan

My boss sometimes forwards me emails with attachments from his phone. Without fail, every time, he manages to duplicate the attachment exactly so there are 2 copies of the same attachment on the email. I can't for the life of me figure out how he manages to do this. #Boomerfail

@KyleSeever 21 Nov

I saw an article on side hustles with a comment, 'WHY ARE ALL THESE MILLENNIALS FOCUSED ON SIDE HUSTLES AND NOT A FULL-TIME JOB?' Maybe because you ruined the economy and strapped us with DEBILITATING STUDENT DEBT and we can BARELY AFFORD TO LIVE ON ONE JOB, CAROL. #OKBoomer

@ChristinePiela 2 Feb

I deserve an award. A patient kept asking the same nonsense question over & over again & when I asked him to clarify he went 'How do you not understand?? You must be a millennial.' It took all of my willpower not to snap back with an 'OK Boomer'.

@giselle_leos 1 Feb

AVOIDED SAYING "OK BOOMER" AT WORK

Highlight of my work week was sitting in 1-hour training about how saying 'OK Boomer' is harassment. **@squidnei 30 Jan**

Another baby boomer at work looked at the TATTOO ON MY ARM and said 'YOU KNOW THOSE ARE PERMANENT RIGHT?' and I said 'NO.'

@deelalz 31 Aug

New theory:
#Boomers blame #Millennials for quitting so much as a way to mask the fact that they have poor people management skills.

@redneckjonathan 4 Feb

Alexa, why does a baby boomer who doesn't read emails, won't update their browser version and can't rotate a PDF, make triple my salary?

@tony_charm 24 Jul

Good news for people with graphic design-adjacent skills: there will always be jobs for us as long as Boomers refuse to learn how to open PDFs and save things as jpegs.

@KerinCunningham 24 Jan

A co-worker asked me to look up something online. When I asked where to go, she said 'YouTubeDOTCOM' OK Boomer.

@Jandalize 16 Jan

Called my boss a Boomer today and got fired smh

@dam3xx 15 Jan

Boomers be like 'Tattoos? Ha. Unemployable! Now let me get back to tolerating workplace sexual harassment because that is normal and fine.'

@molly7anne 23 Aug

Baby Boomer:
Walk in to ask if they're hiring, the manager will respect the initiative!

Employee you ask:
Oh yeah, just go home and apply online.

@lizzylemondrop 7 Jun

6

SCHOOL DAYS

Teaching is tough.

Are you trying to broaden the minds of the younger generation? Sorry, but you're a prime OK Boomer target.

Are you a student? Depending on how young your parents are, this may be your first interaction with a Boomer.

Remember, they hold the keys to your good grades and bright future (even though it feels like they are the ones who have a lot to learn), so tread carefully …

Officially hate this class where the prof believes our generation 'lacks resilience' and 'has too much emotional instability' and that's why we have high rates of depression and su*cide lmao OK BOOMER

@AleianaZelin 4 Feb

Boomer in my letter press class asked if 'OK Boomer' had an exclamation point and I said no, but that adding one would be the most Boomer thing he could do. He said he was reclaiming the boom.

@KristinGeorgeB 19 Jan

I want to fucking die. My 60-year-old professor is having trouble with the projector and google drive and he's fumbling around. Then he said 'OK Boomer' to himself when he figured it out.

@_tamwah 16 Jan

Today I was working with a 1st grader on a math problem and I told him that he had the wrong answer, and then he had the audacity to say 'OK BOOMER' like he didn't believe me. #HEATED

@mumm_aaron 15 Jan

I told my little brother to do his homework and he really hit me with an 'OK Boomer'. I don't know whether to be mad or proud.

@laurenn_hanlon 29 Jan

My professor was doing a lecture about age demographics and he said the word 'boomer' at least 30 times without ever making an 'OK Boomer' joke. I'm so proud of him.

@Schaffrillas 30 Jan

One of my 5th graders said 'OK BOOMER' in response to something I said and then asked if whiteboards had been invented when I was a kid so I'm really not sure if the kids are, in fact, alright.

@shirawolkenfeld 26 Jan

Having a professor who's a baby boomer encourage the phrase 'OK Boomer' and call out the ignorance of her generation has become my favorite part of this semester.

@Melinanuttall 24 Jan

My 11 year olds have gotten into the habit of saying 'OK Boomer' every time I discipline them in class ... I'm 27.

@kchristianv 13 Feb

Boomers: They should teach kids how to balance a check book instead of art.
Me: They should teach kids the yoga moves that alleviate back pain caused by computer jobs instead of baseball.

<u>@weedguy420boner 26 Jan</u>

7

CUSTOMER SERVICE

Nothing annoys a Boomer at quite the same velocity as poor customer service. It's *fascinating* to watch.

Having been able to sail through their education without the need for a part-time job, many Boomers are unfamiliar with the complexities of hospitality work.

They have taken the philosophy of 'The customer is always right' to *extreme* levels.

My Baby
Boomer parents:
Millennials are
whiny babies.

Also my Baby
Boomer parents:
*Leaves 800-
word Yelp review
cuz of cold fries
at Chili's*

@ValeeGrrl 10 Apr

Me: 'OK Boomer' is hilarious but I don't think I'd ever actually say it to someone.

Customer who ASKED for my help: I don't need a millennial to tell me how to do my own damn job.

Me:

<u>@yoPeppy 23 Jan</u>

Me:
Sorry we're out of that, it's been a busy day.

Millennial, understanding stock can diminish:
No problem at all.

Baby Boomer:

@shauntae_stay 7 Aug

Barista:
What can I get you?

Boomer: In my day we had to grind the beans with our teeth.

Barista: OK.

Boomer: We boiled water with hard work and boot straps.

Barista: Cool, so can I get you anything?

Boomer: Venti half caf soy latte extra whip 6 pumps of vanilla.

@Tryptofantastic 29 Jan

Accidentally had an airpod in when dealing with a customer and he got mad at me so I told him it was a hearing aid and he apologized. Dumb ass boomer

@leslieejimenez 7 Dec

Someone said that your customer service voice is just baby talk for Boomers and I can't get over that.

@_kylandia 2 Dec

Me:
Sorry we're closed
Millennial:
Oh, I'm sorry lol
Baby Boomer:
WE HAVE 2 FULL MINUTES LEFT, U CAN'T REFUSE SERVICE, CUSTOMER'S ALWAYS RIGH–

@rainymondays 5 Mar

Older people say our generation is soft and then complain that the young waitress working her ass off doesn't clear tables fast enough for them to get a table in 30 seconds. #OKBoomer

@myoungblood89 2 Feb

This old dude who just complained about the absence of plastic lids AT A VEGAN STAND was tryna throw hands with me and the worker goes 'OK Boomer' LOL

@joey_shoaf 3 Feb

Today an older customer was very friendly and understanding while I worked with him.

He was an OK BOOMER.

@whichdeer 9 Dec

8

BUT I'M A MILLEN—

For non-baby boomers, being on the receiving end of an 'OK Boomer' can shock you to your core. We know, it stings.

You look at the young whippersnapper in front of you and think 'How could they? Don't they know how young I am?'

The sad truth is, Boomer is in the eye of the beholder. You just have to suppress your emotions and take it on the chin like a true Boomer.

You *can*, however, be comforted by the fact that one day *they* will be considered Boomers too.

BIRTH TO AGE 30:
YOU'RE TOO YOUNG
TO HAVE AN OPINION
WORTH TAKING
SERIOUSLY.
AGE 30 TO DEATH:
OK BOOMER.

@OLIVERJIA1014 24 JAN

SOMEDAY 'OK BOOMER'
IS GOING TO TURN
INTO 'OK MILLENNIAL'
AND I AM SO NOT
READY FOR THAT.

@_VAMPIEGIRL 25 JAN

Raise your hand if you're tired of explaining 'OK Boomer' to Boomers who think it's as bad as a racist slur and gen x'rs who are like I wAs BoRn iN 1974 tHaT doesn't eVen MakE sEnSe??!?!!

If Gen Z is Zoomers and Baby Boomers are Boomers, does that make Millennials Moomers? I am a Moomer #moomer #OKBoomer

@haddon_nate 2 Jan

EVERYONE OLDER
THAN ME IS A BABY
BOOMER AND
EVERYONE YOUNGER
THAN ME IS A BABY

@keyawn 9 Mar

A 10-YEAR-OLD OK
BOOMER'D ME OVER
THE HOLIDAYS.
*PROMPTLY PURCHASES
NEW EYE CREAM*

@CarisaNietsche 18 Jan

Someone said 'OK Boomer' to me today and I've never been so offended. I'm not even 21.

@_Katty_x 30 Jan

Me in my 20s:
Goes out 5 nights a week, no issue, no hangovers, just living life

Me in my 30s:
Goes out one night out of the week, in bed the next day by 9:30pm like #OKBoomer

@AshleyElisaG 19 Jan

Ten years ago I would have been excited because it's the weekend. Today I'm excited because we rearranged the furniture in the living room. #fml #OKBoomer

@jeffcarmack 1 Feb

I did it. I said the old fartiest thing I have ever said to date: 'Oh remember this song' ... *sings some lyrics* ... 'I think I had this on CD single' #OKBoomer #Millennial #ThatOld #CDs

@Missavrilxxx 31 Jan

9

MONEY

Money makes the world go round ... but here's a graph that explains what has happened to money:

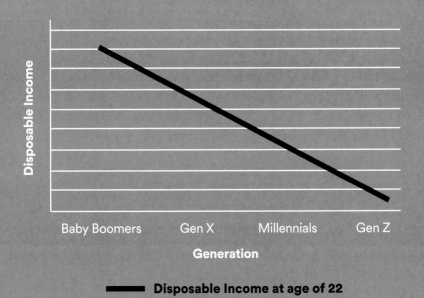

Grandad: YOUR GENERATION IS SO SPOILED Me: *FLIPPING COIN* HEADS I PAY RENT, TAILS I EAT

@robots_feel 14 Jan

U OWN A HOME? OK Boomer

@nick_lindquist 29 Jan

Average Day in the Life of a Baby Boomer:

– Wake up
– Have coffee
– Read a print newspaper
– Eat an English muffin
– Become overwhelmed with an intense desire to write a passionate defence of Woody Allen
– Drive PT Cruiser to work

@KrangTNelson 11 Feb

Boomers:
You get more conservative as you get older.

Me at 17:
Let the gays marry!

Me at 27:
We must eliminate all billionaires, guns & prisons, then use their money to create true wealth equality while protecting the planet and all marginalised groups.

@neonfiona 27 Jan

Boomers: I can't wait to buy a summer house
Gen Z: I would love to one day own a desk

@honeybeetrice 25 Nov

Millennials are so spoiled with their tablets and smartphones. All our parents had at this age was the ability to buy property in most major metropolitan areas in the United States.

@BenRaynor4 21 Nov

🤦 GOT IN A DISCUSSION WITH MY PARENTS ABOUT FREE COLLEGE AND THEY WENT ON A RANT ABOUT HOW IN THEIR DAY THEY WORKED HARD AND PAID FOR COLLEGE THEMSELVES. **#OKBOOMER** LITERALLY DID NOT BELIEVE ME WHEN I SAID THAT IS NOT POSSIBLE TODAY.

@MrsWendySue 5 Feb

If I had $1 for every time a baby boomer asked me if I paid to have rips in my shorts, I'd have enough money to fix the economy they destroyed.

@a24manda 25 May

10

FAMILY LIFE

If you have a Boomer in the home, you've probably developed a high tolerance to their confusing remarks, but occasionally, the *level* of Boomerism that comes out of their mouth can surprise you. And you just.

My dad refers to any podcast, media outlet, online publication, and YouTube channel I watch or listen to as a 'blog' #OKBoomer

@thirstygrrl 4 Feb

My mom is reading the book 'The Subtle Art of Not Giving a Fuck' and I'm dying cause she has been chirping my not giving a fuck attitude for 25 yrs #OKBoomer

@AmazonMma 11 Feb

www.OKBoomer.com

MY MOM JUST CALLED TO ASK ABOUT OK BOOMER … SHE THOUGHT IT WAS A WEBSITE WHERE PEOPLE GO TO MAKE FUN OF BOOMERS

@JeffKasanoff 17 Jan

SETS ALL OF MY DAD'S CLOCKS BACK ONE HOUR
ME: LATE BOOMER

@professorkiosk 25 Jan

I've never once been tempted to say 'OK Boomer' but my mom is one of those people who gets her opinions from Facebook and has just been reading aloud some post about how actually the younger generations are to blame for the climate crisis and I swear to god I almost said it 💀

@waywardliliana 25 Jan

Dads be like, I put a ROOF over your HEAD. OK Boomer, u could've also just worn a condom

@literallysofie 3 Feb

**My aunt:
Your online friends are not REAL friends, it is NOT considered social interaction or anything of that sort
Me:
OK Boomer**

@Hiyarii_ 28 Jan

I jokingly yelled 'that ain't it sis' at my 9yo and she fired back 'OK Boomer' so I guess this is my life now.

@CCBraves 4 Feb

WHEN YOUR DAD USES TWITTER INSTEAD OF A TEXT TO BROADCAST HIS NEWS AND REVEAL YOUR CHILDHOOD NICKNAME TO THE WORLD #BOOMERFAIL #GLOBALNEWS

@REANNABROWNE 20 OCT

Thinking about when my 12yo brother OK Boomer'd me yesterday

@nishihiruhh 9 Dec

My six year old: Pluto's not a planet.

**Me:
He was in my day.**

**#BackInMyDay
#OKBoomer**

@muhlegshurt 5 Feb

My child's first words after being born were 'OK Boomer'

@4ever_a_loam 18 Jan

I fear that a lot of us will end up having #OKBoomer engraved on our headstones

@Faux_Schlmoe 30 Jan

11

CULTURE

It's not until you start looking at the world through a Boomer lens that you realise, they truly are *everywhere*. Films, TV shows, books, song lyrics, the Royal Family ... we could go on.

So, like you would during an Oscars montage sequence, kick back and take a look over some of our favourite Boomer moments (loosely) embedded within pop culture ...

Darth Vader: If you only knew the power of the dark side
Luke: OK Boomer

@steeve_again 13 Oct

Luke: I failed you Ben, I'm sorry
Kylo: OK Boomer

@mandyspaghetti 27 Jan

Thanos: I am inevitable
Iron Man: OK Boomer

@Peku14 14 Nov

RON:
OK BOOMER

DUMBLEDORE:
SON I AM OLD ENOUGH TO BE A BOOMER'S GRANDAD, DON'T YOU SASS ME

#ronweasley
#albusdumbledore

@Accio-shitpost 17 jan

A STUDENT OK BOOMER'D ME.

I HAD TO EXPLAIN THAT I'M GEN X, AND WHAT A BOOMER IS.

SHE THEN OK MUGGLE'D ME.

THEN I CORRECTED HER THAT I'M SLYTHERIN.

SHE GAVE UP.

@Marisabillions 29 jan

Marcus aurelius, around 170 AD: you always own the option of having no opinion.

Twitter, 2020: lol fuck that guy, OK Boomer.

@willmoriarty86 21 Jan

My daughter
is reading 'the
merchant of venice'
in 8th grade english
and tonight she told
me, 'OUT UPON IT,
OLD CARRION' is
shakespeare for
'OK BOOMER'.
Teenagers are the
goddamn best.

@HeidiStevens13 14 Jan

A STUDENT'S TAKE ON THE READINGS:

Burke:
The French Revolution is terrible! Chivalry is dead!

Wollstonecraft:
OK Boomer

@sallydemarest 2 Feb

Apparently I just had my #OKBoomer moment. Someone jokingly said I'm so old I'd even ask 'Who's Billie Eilish?' and I answered with 'I don't, who is he?'

@RalphJanik 31 Jan

I just accidentally said LinkedIn Park while referring to the band #OKBoomer

@colemartian 10 Dec

**Boomers:
Where are all the
politicised pop stars?
The Dylan, the Lennon,
the Strummer of today?
In my time, musicians
had something to say.**

**Stormzy:
Britain is racist**

**Boomers:
Shut up you uppity thug!
Stick to rapping, no one
wants to hear you speak
on politics.**

@KojoKoram 22 Dec

Harry and Meghan: We quit the royal family.
Queen Elizabeth: Fucking Millennials.
Harry and Meghan: OK Boomer.

@RiotGrlErin 8 Jan

Let's change the lyrics to 'you scumbag, you maggot, you cheap lousy boomer' and see who the snowflakes are, yeah?

@shckldg 26 Dec

12

DON'T DISH IT OUT IF YOU CAN'T TAKE IT

Here's a fun pie chart.

Boomers who find
'OK Boomer' offensive

Boomers who use the word
'Snowflake' to describe anyone
younger than them

'stoP mAkINg fuN OF BOOmERS'

Why? What are they gonna do? Bankrupt the economy, cut their own taxes, start two endless wars, kill the environment, outsource manufacturing jobs, usher in a new age of fascism, and make it impossible to buy a house or pay for college? **OK Boomer**

@jules_su 4 Nov

Boomers:
Blame Millennials for everything and make fun of a whole generation
Millennials: H—
Boomers: Shut up, you need to learn! We are older than you!
Gen Z: *Decides to make fun of Boomers with just 'OK Boomer'*
Boomers: HOW DARE YOU?! HOW SAD! SO DISRESPECTFUL

@lauraherself 30 Oct

Boomers:

Call Gen Z stupid

Boomers:

Call Gen Z sensitive

Boomers:

Call Gen Z snowflakes

Boomers:

Call Gen Z –

Gen Z:

OK Boomer

Boomers:

They can call you a 'good for nothing snowflake millennial' all day but you say 'OK Boomer' once and next thing you know you're in time out for being disrespectful.

@Strain44 11 Feb

New rule: If a baby boomer calls you lazy or implies your generation is lazy, refuse to help them when they need you to fix their router.

@elizabethdanger 15 May

13

NO BOOMER, JUST NO

Here is a celebration of
the very best of the worst
Boomerisms.

The ones who are too far gone
to save.

These End-of-Level Bad
Boomers may make us grind
our teeth in rage, but at least
they give us something to
laugh about/roll our eyes at ...

So me and my guy friend were walking at the beach yesterday and I put a flower in his hair, then an old guy walked by and said to us, 'I think the wrong person is wearing that flower' ... OK BOOMER IT'S 2020, flower boys are the VIBE

@Vanessa_Murrayy 26 Jan

Do not ask people when they are getting married or having kids. Find your own happiness and leave others alone. #OKBoomer

@AnnW_McC 2 Feb

I woke up this morning and saw a bird of prey in my backyard eating avocado toast and yelling 'OK Boomer!' It was a millennial falcon.

@NorthernOvation 31 Jan

There was a little boy with a ladybird backpack in a shop earlier, & a baby boomer made a snide comment about it being 'girly'. He immediately turned around and came back with 'ladybirds squirt acid from their knees like a xenomorph'.
That kid is going places.
#babyboomers

@WheelsofSteer 28 Aug

I got told my generation is nothing but 'know-it-all assholes' at the gym today by some old ass man because he asked me how I TURNED A TV ON and I said 'I literally just hit the power button' OK Boomer

@LoganMerrill4L 21 Jan

Somebody replied to a tweet where I said 'OK Boomer' by saying 'OK Twerp' and I can't think of a more Boomer insult than the word 'Twerp'

@NostromoSerg 30 Jan

Boomers:
I heard she went to ... *looks around nervously and whispers* ... Therapy

Millennials/Gen Z:
LMAOOOO YALL GUESS WHAT MY THERAPIST TOLD ME TODAY

@jordylancaster 25 Jul

I had a customer tell me today she's never listening to or supporting Jay-Z and Beyoncé ever again because they sat during the national anthem and it was 'SO BAD'. OK Boomer

@abeazyy 3 Feb

So far I've learned that people over the age of 35 don't know how to control their flashlights on their phones #notinmyeyes #okboomer

@torri_huebner 5 Feb

Had someone chat with me about hunting and said he had a taxidermied polar bear he'd taken out. That's the most #OKBoomer energy I've ever experienced. Hunting something you eat is fine, but how tf do you justify hunting a polar bear?

@miltag 2 Feb

Polar Bear

14

BYE BYE BOOMER, BOOMER BYE BYE

There may well come a time when 'OK Boomer' is lost and forgotten.

No doubt there will be a digital war soon, so perhaps this book will be the only proof it existed at all. You may be reading this in the year 3000 in a museum behind a glass box. If they still have museums by then ...

Anyway, it's hard to imagine a time when nobody is saying 'OK Boomer', but this chapter gives us a glimpse into the future ...

If I know my internet cultural cycles, now that 'boomer' has become a widely used pejorative, we're weeks away from boomers co-opting it and wearing shirts with bald eagles and American flags on them saying You Can't Spell Patriot Without Boomer or whatever.

@InternetHippo 31 Oct

I HOPE THE USAGE OF 'OK BOOMER' DOESN'T BECOME CLICHÉ BECAUSE I REALLY NEED THAT GO-TO WAY TO REACT TO STUPID OLD PEOPLE.

@its_crowley 4 Feb

WHAT DO YOU CALL IT WHEN SOMEONE SAYS 'OK BOOMER' AND SOMEONE SAYS IT RIGHT BACK TO THEM?
AN OK BOOMERANG.
SORRY. TOO MUCH WINE.
I'LL SEE MYSELF OUT.

@BridgetSterli19 24 Jan

Damn we have depleted the finite comic resource of 'OK Boomer' with alarming speed and no eye to sustainability. Who's the boomer now?

@BrandyLJensen 5 Nov

ACKNOWLEDGEMENTS

Many thanks to the authors of these posts. Every effort has been made to credit the authors; please contact the publishers with any corrections.